PLAY and LEARN

with your 6 year old

63 simple activities

Learn while having fun

Quality time for parents and children

The activities in this book are organized into the following sections:

Special thanks to Joan Henry and Jean Tuemmler, my Mulberry Tree teaching team.

Congratulations on your purchase of some of the finest teaching materials in the world.

For information about other Evan-Moor products, call 1-800-777-4362 or FAX 1-800-777-4332

Visit our website http://www.evan-moor.com. Check the Product Updates link for supplements, additions, and corrections for this book.

Author:	Jill Norris
Editor:	Marilyn Evans
Copy Editor:	Cathy Harber
Illustrator:	Cindy Davis
Designer:	Cheryl Puckett
Desktop:	Carolina Caird
Cover:	Cheryl Puckett

Evan-Moor
EDUCATIONAL PUBLISHERS
EMC 4505

How to Play and Learn with Your Six-Year-Old

What can I do to help my six-year-old learn and have fun at the same time? This book answers that question with 63 simple activities that parents can do as they spend quality time with their children. Each activity is fun *and* provides a positive learning experience.

Use this book as a resource. Read over the activities to become familiar with them, but don't worry about doing them precisely. Enjoy the special time you spend with your child. Remember that each child is a unique individual. As your child approaches and moves through six, you may notice:

Six-year-olds can be the center of their own universe.

Recognize the egocentricity of your six-year-old. Accept his or her need to be first and best. Understand your child's need for developing independence and maintaining close relationships at the same time.

Six-year-olds can want it all.

Some six-year-olds seem to contradict themselves. They want both of any two opposites. They find it hard to make a choice, but once the choice has been made, they may immediately have an overpowering need for its opposite. Having the biggest piece is important to six-year-olds.

Six-year-olds can be lively intellectually.

As your child gains maturity and independence, encourage new activities that take advantage of these characteristics. Provide opportunities that include setting up an experiment, counting, reading, and playing guessing games. Enjoy new adventures together.

Most of your child's early learning comes from play. During play your child:
- develops and practices skills.
- learns about new ideas and explores new places.
- makes connections between concrete things and abstract ideas.

Building Blocks to Learning

Be Positive

Children are sensitive to criticism. Praise your child whenever you can. Anticipate problem situations and plan for them. Help your child to feel successful.

Appreciate Creativity

Provide the materials and praise that will encourage your child's creative spirit. Applaud the creative process, not only the product. Challenge your child to look at things in new ways.

Talk, Listen, and Read

Many children love to talk. They ask for information, tell about their experiences, and make their own generalizations. Reinforce their language use by talking and listening to them. Listen as your child plays matching word games, creates crazy rhymes, learns the sounds that different letters make, and reads.

Skills for Success

Each page in *Play and Learn* is labeled to tell which skill areas are developed by the activity. Often a single activity addresses several different skills. You help to build the foundation for your child's success in school when you provide practice in these six important skills:

 Large-Motor Development
walking, running, jumping, large-muscle movement

 Coordination and Dexterity
small-muscle movements in the hands and fingers

 Language Development
speaking, listening, and developing vocabulary

 Creativity
imagining, exploring different materials, thinking in new ways

 Problem Solving
finding alternative solutions, understanding cause and effect

 Memory and Concentration
remembering, connecting different ideas

Art Time

Draw, paint,
Cut, paste —
A flying mouse.

Saw, sand,
Nail, drill —
A new birdhouse.

I love to see the things I do
Valued, used, and put out to view.

Play and Learn to

- encourage creativity
- learn about the properties and qualities of materials
- build sense of independence
- develop imagination
- sharpen perceptions
- improve small- and large-motor coordination

Activities

A Pop-Up Card

**Make this card for any special occasion and then send it.
Your six-year-old will be a proud artist and creator.**

What You Need

- two 1" x 12" (2.5 x 30.5 cm) strips of construction paper
- 6" x 8" (15 x 20 cm) piece of colored construction paper
- drawings of flowers or animals—Have your child create these. Crayon, pencil, marker, paint, or computer drawings will work.
- glue
- scissors

What You Do

1. Fold the piece of construction paper in half to make the card.

2. Decorate the front of the card with the drawings. Save one drawing for the pop-up inside the card.

3. Glue the ends of the construction paper strips at right angles. Fold the strips back and forth across the glued end. This is called a catspring.

4. Glue the catspring inside the card.

5. Glue the reserved drawing to the end of the catspring.

6. Add words to the card. Write the words as your child dictates them, or let your child write his or her own message.

7. Put the card in an envelope. An envelope adds "value" to the card and makes it special.

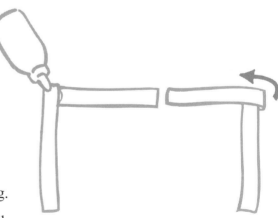

Be sure to acknowledge the artist with a byline on the back of the card. "This card created especially for you by Amy."

Cookie-Cutter Prints

Your child will enjoy creating the paper you use to wrap gifts or cover books.

What You Need

- tempera paint—2 or 3 colors
- cookie cutters
- brown paper bag
- small paper plate
- newspaper or drop cloth

What You Do

1. Prepare painting area. Spread out newspapers or drop cloth on a flat surface. You may want to put newspaper on the floor as well.

2. Pour a puddle of paint on the paper plate.

3. Cut the brown bag open and lay it flat on the painting area.

4. Dip a cookie cutter into the puddle of paint.

5. Press the painted edge on the brown paper.

6. Dip and press to decorate the brown paper.

7. Let the paper dry. Cut to the desired size and use. Cover a book or a pencil can. Wrap a gift or laminate to use as a placemat.

Rubbing Magic

Crayon rubbings delight six-year-olds because they seem to appear magically. Do some rubbings indoors or outdoors and then compare the different pictures that you've created.

What You Need

- white paper
- old crayons
- paper shapes (optional)

What You Do

1. Take the paper wrappers off the crayons.

2. Lay the white paper on a textured surface or over a flat object.
   - leaf
   - wood shingle
   - paper shape
   - paving rock

3. Hold the crayon on its side and rub it over the surface of the paper. Keep rubbing until an image appears.

4. Move the paper to a new surface or place a different object beneath the paper. Repeat the process.

5. Talk with your child about the rubbings that you have made.
   How are they alike?
   How are they different?

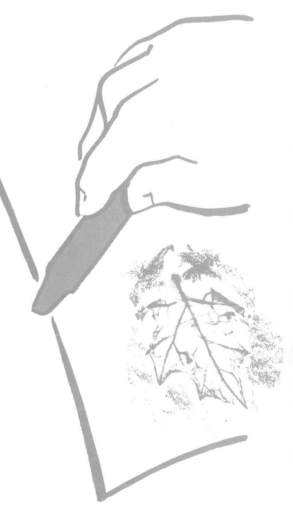

> Use cutout letters under the paper to spell names and messages.

New Goo

Make this wonderful stuff and experience changes that occur in materials when they are combined. This is squishy fun!

What You Need

- liquid starch
- white glue
- small widemouthed container with lid, such as a yogurt container
- small bowl

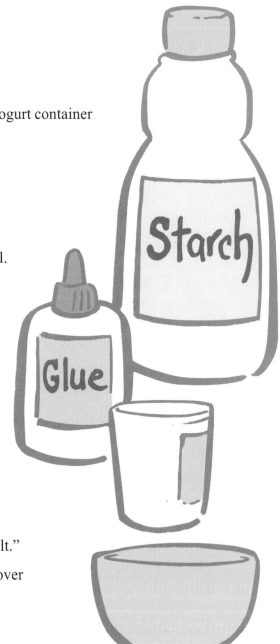

What You Do

1. Put 2 tablespoons (30 ml) of starch into the bowl.

2. Add 2 tablespoons (30 ml) of white glue. Wait for five minutes.

3. Stir with a spoon until globs form. Don't worry if there is some starch left in the bowl.

4. Knead the globs in your hands. This is part of the fun. At first the globs will be stringy and slimey. As you knead, the globs will form one smooth mass. Knead at least 5 minutes.

5. Play with the new goo!
   - Mold the mass into a snake. Hold the two ends and watch it sag.
   - Fold the goo and mash it to make it pop.
   - Lay the goo in your hand and watch it "melt."

6. Store the goo in an airtight container and use it over and over.

Watercolor Resist

Combine two familiar mediums as you paint over crayon drawings.

What You Need

- crayons
- paper
- watercolor paint
- fat brush
- water

What You Do

1. Draw a picture using the crayons.

2. Saturate your brush with water.

3. Dip the wet brush into the watercolor paint.

4. Paint over the crayon drawing.
   Make long strokes across the whole page.
   Do not paint over your initial strokes.
   It's fine if some places on the page
   are not covered by paint.

I have two framed watercolor resists hanging in my living room. They are bright, beautiful, and always a topic of conversation. My son did both when he was six!

Box Puzzle

Create a collection of three-dimensional puzzles that your child can enjoy putting together. Let your child help with the assembly.

What You Need

- 4 small cardboard boxes (Pudding or gelatin boxes work well.)
- picture (your child's photo, drawing, or a picture cut from a magazine)
- glue
- spray paint
- tape

What You Do

Preparing the Boxes

1. Tape the empty boxes closed.
2. Spray paint the boxes on all sides. Let them dry completely.

Making the Puzzle

1. Use a drawing or photo smaller than the area of the four boxes placed together.
2. Cut the picture into fourths.
3. Arrange the boxes to create a square.
4. Lay the picture on top of the boxes so that the pieces fit together.
5. Glue the drawing pieces to the boxes.
6. Turn the boxes over and repeat with another drawing.

Special Tees

**Decorate T-shirts using fabric crayons and three-dimensional paint.
Then enjoy wearing "special tees."**

What You Need

• prewashed cotton T-shirt

• fabric crayons (Buy them at a craft or fabric store.)

• three-dimensional paint (such as Puffy Paint®)

• iron

• piece of cardboard

• paper

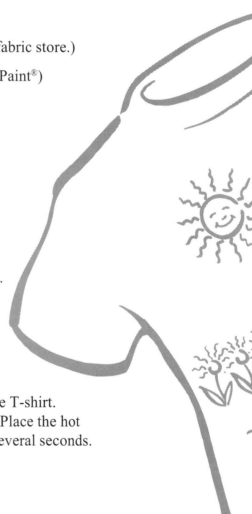

What You Do

1. Draw pictures with the fabric crayons.

2. Transfer the pictures to the T-shirt.
    • Slip the piece of cardboard inside the T-shirt to prevent color from going through the layers of fabric.
    • Lay the picture facedown on the T-shirt.
    • **Adult supervision required**—Place the hot iron on the picture. Leave for several seconds.
    • Remove the iron.
    • Remove the paper.

3. Allow the T-shirt to cool.

4. Decorate the transferred pictures with three-dimensional paint. Add dots, outlines, special features, and stripes.

5. Wear the new T-shirt proudly.

Color Bursts

Watch colors combine and change as coffee filters are dipped into food coloring.

What You Need

- round basket-type coffee filters
- food coloring
- muffin tin

What You Do

1. In the four corners of a muffin tin, mix food coloring with water. (Experiment with the intensity until you are happy with the color the solution makes. Start with four drops of food coloring and one tablespoon [15 ml] of water.)

2. Open the coffee filter flat. Fold it in half several times.

3. Dip each corner of the folded filter into a different food-color solution. Dip in and out of the color quickly—the coloring moves fast.

4. Unfold the filter and dry.

Display color bursts on a door or decorate a window with the bright circles of color.

Baker's Clay

Baker's clay is a flexible clay that holds its shape well. Encourage your child to explore the clay by rolling, flattening, pinching, and cutting.

What You Need

- bowl
- spoon
- 4 cups (500 g) of flour
- 1 cup (288 g) of salt
- 1½ cups (360 ml) of warm water

What You Do

1. Make the baker's clay with your child.
   - Dissolve the salt in the warm water.
   - Stir as you add the flour to the salt-water mixture.
   - Knead the dough until it is pliable, at least five minutes.

2. Roll, flatten, pinch, cut, coil, and shape the baker's clay.

3. If you want to preserve your creations, bake at 300°–350° F (150°–175° C) until hard. (The baking time will depend on the thickness and size of the project.)

A Baker's Clay Snail

Here's a simple project to make using baker's clay.

What You Need

- baker's clay
- pencil
- small container of water
- cookie sheet
- colored markers
- clear gloss spray finish

What You Do

1. Start with two walnut-sized balls of clay.

2. Roll one ball into a long "snake."

3. Form the snake into a coil for the snail shell.

4. Roll the other ball into a flat oval to form the snail's body.

5. Moisten the bottom of the shell and the center of the body with water. Set the shell on the body and press gently to attach.

6. Roll the "head" up. Poke 2 holes for eyes with a pencil point.

7. Bake in a 300° F (150° C) oven until hard.

8. Optional: Use colored markers to paint the snail's shell. Spray with clear gloss finish.

Clay from Bread

Enjoy a different clay experience using two slices of bread and some white glue. The type of bread that you use will determine the clay's texture.

What You Need

- two slices of bread
- two tablespoons (30 ml) of white glue
- small bowl
- acrylic paints
- glossy acrylic spray finish

What You Do

1. Trim the crusts from the bread and tear it into tiny pieces.

2. Using your hands, mix the white glue into the bread. It will be very sticky at first, but will become claylike as you knead it.

3. Shape the clay. It is easier to do this if you divide the clay into balls and then pinch these balls into animal figures or tiny dishes. Keep the shapes simple.

4. Air dry your creations or bake them in the oven. The temperature should be set between 200º F (95º C) and 300º F (150º C). You will need to check the sculptures regularly. The size and thickness of each piece will determine its baking time.

5. Paint the pieces with acrylic paints.

6. Spray each piece with a coat of glossy acrylic finish.

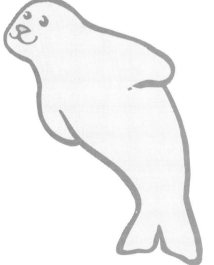

Mealtime

I made a list.
I read it through.
I knew just what
I had to do.

I'm learning how
To write and read.
So I can shop
For what I need.

Menu Memoboard

Create a special memoboard in your kitchen for your child. Then use it to post upcoming menus, special requests, and picture recipes for make-by-yourself snacks.

What You Need

- a rectangle of brown paper bag or gift wrap, the size you would like your memoboard to be

- small magnets

- set of magnetic letters

- pad of self-adhesive notes

What You Do

1. Put the paper rectangle on a metal surface in your kitchen—the door of your refrigerator, the side of your stove, the water cooler. The square should be at your child's eye level. Hold it in place with magnets or tape.

2. Give the memoboard a name. Write the name on the board with the magnetic letters (for example, "Norris News").

3. Post picture recipes, requests for lunches, and shopping lists. See the next page for two recipes you might use.

At our house the board was also used as a reminder of upcoming events, a convenient spot to post messages, and a practice board for writing words. All three of my children used the magnetic letters to write words and messages as I worked in the kitchen.

Picture Recipes for Your Memoboard

Fruit Salad

1. Lettuce leaf
2. Peanut butter
3. Raisins
4. Roll it up.
5. Eat!

Bagel Bite

1. Minibagel
2. Honey butter
3. Banana slices
4. Eat!

Food Fractions

Prepare and share food together. As you divide the food, talk about fractions.

What You Need

- food that is easily divided into equal parts—have several "wholes" available

What You Do

1. Decide on a piece of food to share. (a piece of string cheese)

2. Explain that you will divide the food in two pieces—one piece for your child and one piece for you.

3. Divide the food into two pieces. Make one much bigger than the other. Give the smaller piece to your child and keep the larger piece. Your child will probably react.
   Your piece is bigger than mine!
   If not, encourage your child to compare the two pieces by asking,
   How's your piece?
   Are the two pieces the same size?

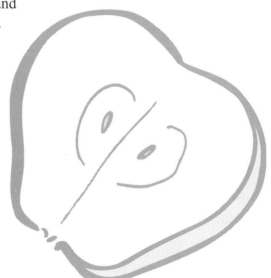

4. Divide another whole, this time into halves. Compare the pieces with your child. Say,
   *When a whole thing is divided into equal-sized pieces, the pieces have a special name. The pieces are called **fractions**. When a whole thing is divided into two equal-sized pieces we call the fractions **halves**.*

5. Let your child divide the next whole into halves.
   - Point out other wholes that have been divided into pieces. These might include pizza, cinnamon rolls in a pan, and watermelon slices.
   - Talk about whether the pieces are fractions (pieces of equal size) or not.
   - Gradually introduce different fraction names—fourths, thirds, eighths.

Play and Learn with Your Six-Year-Old • EMC 4505

Print Placemats

Using familiar print from advertisements and food packaging, create placemats with your child. Then read the placemats as you eat.

What You Need

- large piece of construction paper
- trademarks and words that your child recognizes
- glue
- clear contact paper

What You Do

1. Trim the paper into a placemat shape.

2. Cut trademarks and words from advertisements, magazines, and newspapers.

3. Glue the words to the paper.

4. Sandwich the placemat between two pieces of clear contact paper.

5. Use the new placemat proudly.

Your child may want to dictate or write a message on the placemat.
I can read the words around me!

Fancy Toast

Combine your child's creative and culinery talents to make this tasty treat.

What You Need

- 2 slices of white bread
- food coloring
- milk
- muffin pan
- cotton-tipped swabs
- toaster

What You Do

1. Pour a little milk into several cups of the muffin pan.

2. Color each cup of milk a different color using a few drops of food coloring.

3. Using the cotton-tipped swabs and the colored milk, "paint" the bread. (Use a different swab for each color.)

4. Dry the paintings by toasting the bread lightly in a toaster.

5. Make sandwiches using your special slices.

Cook with Me!

Prepare a meal together.

What You Need

- small cutting board or work surface
- food ingredients

What You Do

1. Begin by having your child help you do a single step in food preparation. Say,
   Help me stir the batter.

2. Then assign a single independent task.
   - Wash the lettuce leaves.
   - Stir the batter.
   - Cut some fruit.
   - Peel a carrot.
   - Slice the cheese.

3. Finally, have your child prepare a single item. See the recipes on pages 23–25 for ideas.

Green Eggs and Ham

Read the book *Green Eggs and Ham* by Dr. Seuss, make green eggs and ham with your child, and then see if the two of you agree with Sam-I-Am as you eat.

What You Need

- eggs
- precooked, sliced ham
- fork
- frying pan
- blue food coloring
- bowl
- spatula
- nonstick cooking spray

What You Do

1. Help your child break the eggs into the bowl. Stir.

2. Add a few drops of blue food coloring. Stir to mix. (Be sure to note with your child that the eggs turn green as they are stirred.)

3. Spray the frying pan with the cooking spray.

4. Heat the slices of ham in the pan. Move to one side. OR Dice the ham and add it to the green egg mixture.

5. Pour the egg mixture into the pan and cook over medium heat.

6. Stir to scramble.

7. Serve and enjoy.

Do you like green eggs and ham?
My kids and I made this favorite often!

Play and Learn with Your Six-Year-Old • EMC 4505

Cheesy Green Potatoes

Your six-year-old will enjoy eating this baked potato variation, and it's fun to prepare. Let your child do as many steps independently as are appropriate and work together on the rest.

What You Need

- 4 medium potatoes
- bunch of broccoli
- ¾ cup (68 g) of grated cheddar cheese
- 2 tablespoons (28 g) of butter
- 1 teaspoon (6 g) of salt
- ¼ cup (60 ml) of milk

- knife and mixing spoon
- oven mitt
- bowl
- potato masher

What You Do

1. Scrub potatoes. Butter the skins and prick with a fork. Bake in 400° (205° C) oven until done. (Baking time will depend on size of potato.)

2. Cook fresh broccoli and finely chop. (Or use a package of frozen chopped broccoli.)

3. Remove potatoes from oven. Hold the potato with an oven mitt and carefully slice a lengthwise opening.

4. Scoop the insides of the potatoes into a bowl with the broccoli.

5. Add ½ cup (45 g) of cheese, butter, salt, and milk. Mash together until the mixture is pale green with dark green flecks.

6. Heap green mixture back into the potato skins and sprinkle with remaining cheese.

7. Return to the oven to heat through (about 10 minutes).

Play and Learn with Your Six-Year-Old • EMC 4505

Giant Cookies

Wrap these big cookies individually in plastic wrap. The recipe makes twelve 6-inch cookies—big enough for sharing! (Remember those fractions!)

What You Need

- stick of butter (½ cup) or (112 g)
- ¼ cup (48 g) of vegetable shortening
- ½ cup (110 g) of brown sugar
- ½ cup (96 g) of granulated sugar
- 2 eggs
- 2 teaspoons (10 ml) of vanilla
- 1½ cups (188 g) of flour
- ½ teaspoon (2–3 g) each—baking soda, baking powder, salt

- 12-ounce package (340 g) of chocolate chips
- electric mixer or a strong arm
- aluminum foil
- baking sheets
- wire cooling racks

What You Do

1. Cream the butter and the shortening. Beat in the brown sugar and then the white sugar until fluffy.

2. Add the eggs one at a time, beating well after each. Stir in vanilla.

3. Combine flour, baking soda, baking powder, and salt. Stir this flour mixture into the creamed butter and sugar. Blend well.

4. Add the chocolate chips. Mix well.

5. Cover the dough or put it in a plastic bag and chill it completely. (The dough can be left as long as 3 days before baking.)

6. Preheat the oven to 350º F (175º C). Cover the baking sheet with aluminum foil.

7. Scoop fist-size mounds of dough onto the baking sheet. The mounds should be about 3" (7 cm) apart. Flatten the mounds with your hand.

8. Bake the cookies 12–15 minutes. When you remove the cookies from the oven, slide the foil off the baking sheet. Cool the cookies on the foil for 5 minutes. Then move them to wire racks.

Make Your Own Recipe

Provide the ingredients, then stand back and let your child create a new snack.

What You Need

a variety of ingredients, such as:

- apple
- pear
- walnuts
- honey
- coconut
- cinnamon

What You Do

1. Show your child the ingredients that are available.

2. Encourage your child to select from those available and combine them to make a snack.

3. Write down the recipe for your child's creation.

4. Think of a name for the snack.

5. Taste the new creation.

Indoor Playtime

I'm an engineer, a scientist,
A fashion designer, too.
Is there any special work
That I can do for you?

The "work" I do while I play
Helps me learn more every day.

Play and Learn to

- build strong shapes
- see how things work
- learn about magnetism
- measure objects and compare their sizes
- create patterns
- use imagination to solve problems

Activities

Toothpicks and Marshmallows

Learn about strong shapes in this building activity that uses toothpicks and marshmallows.

What You Need

- a bag of miniature marshmallows
- a box of toothpicks
- a flat surface to work on

What You Do

1. Provide the marshmallows and toothpicks and challenge your child to build a house.

2. Work beside your child and build your own house. Make observations about your house as you build.
   This square shape keeps tipping over.
   This tepee seems to stand up without tipping.
   Have you found a shape that stands up by itself?

3. Leave your houses when they are completed and observe the changes that occur. Note the shapes that do not collapse.

4. Try building again using what you've found out about shapes that keep standing. Work together to make a big house.

Newspaper Logs

Roll newspapers into tubes and use the tubes as giant tinkertoys.

What You Need

- sheets of newspaper (Each full sheet makes one log.)
- masking tape
- stapler

What You Do

1. Starting with one corner, roll the newspaper into a tight roll. Secure the corner to the roll with a small piece of masking tape.

2. Make lots of newspaper rolls.

3. Staple the ends of the rolls together to make shapes that stand.
   - Begin by building small triangular lean-to houses for stuffed animals.
   - Work your way up to people-sized huts.

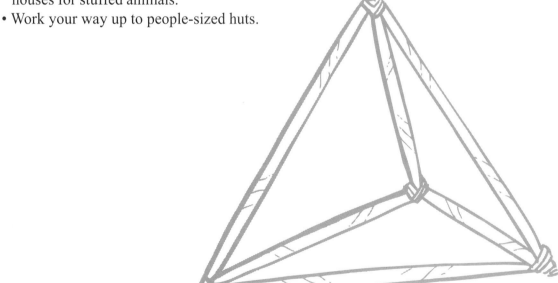

Tiny Tunnels

Three boxes stacked together form an arch. Lots of arches built together form a tunnel.

What You Need

- lots of little cardboard boxes
- tape

What You Do

1. Close the flaps or lids on the boxes. Secure them with a piece of tape.

2. Make a three-box arch.

3. Try a tunnel of three-box arches.
   - Make two parallel rows of boxes close together, but with a space in between them.
   - Add the boxes to form the top.
   - Push a toy car through the tunnel.

Try making a child-size tunnel with larger boxes.

Pick It Up

Try picking up different objects with a magnet, sort the objects into two piles, and then talk about the similarities of the objects in one pile.

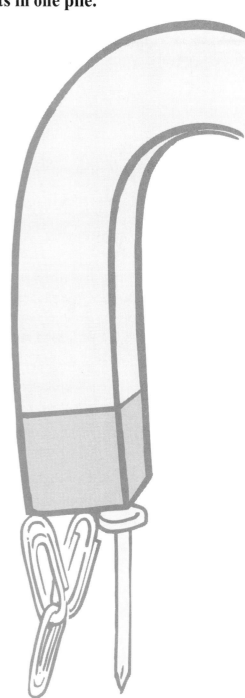

What You Need

- magnet

- everyday objects—pencil, paper clip, tissue, spoon, block, aluminum foil, piece of paper, nail, staple, rock, penny

- 2 baskets or boxes

What You Do

1. Touch the magnet to an object. If the magnet picks the object up, put the object in the "magnetic" basket. If the magnet does not pick up the object, put the object in the "not magnetic" basket.

2. "Test" many objects. Sort them into the two baskets.

3. Look at the objects in the magnetic basket. Say,
   Do all the objects have common characteristics?
   Are they the same shape?
   Are they the same color?
   Are they made of the same materials?

4. Choose a new object. Predict whether it is magnetic or not magnetic by using what you have learned. Test the new object to see if your prediction was accurate.

Take It Apart

Taking an old appliance apart using Mom and Dad's tools is a special treat.

What You Need

- screwdrivers

- pliers

- small appliance with the electrical cord removed
  (Use a broken mixer, a toaster that doesn't work,
  or an old radio. Don't use appliances with sharp edges.)

What You Do

1. Cut or disconnect the electrical cord from a broken or discarded appliance.

2. Give your child permission to take the appliance apart.
   Be sure to explain that this is an activity that can be done
   only with your approval.

3. Provide screwdrivers and pliers. If your child has never used
   tools before, show how they are used.

4. Watch and assist, but let your child take the lead. Ask questions
   that encourage your child to think about the parts of the appliance
   that work together.

5. Lay all the parts together after they are dismantled.
   Encourage your child to record the experience by drawing the
   appliance or naming and labeling its separate parts.

A Growth Chart

Help your child become an informed observer. Noting changes and then measuring to confirm those changes are an important part of the scientific process.

What You Need

- yardstick or tape measure

- scale

- growing thing—plant, pet, bush at the park, baby brother or sister

- notebook or paper for recording observations

What You Do

1. Choose a growing thing to measure.

2. Measure and weigh the thing. Record the date and the measurements in the notebook.

3. Draw a picture or tell about how the thing looks. (You can write what your child dictates.)

4. Make new observations every few days. Be sure to talk about what the observations show.

5. Compare a fast-growing thing to a slow-growing thing.

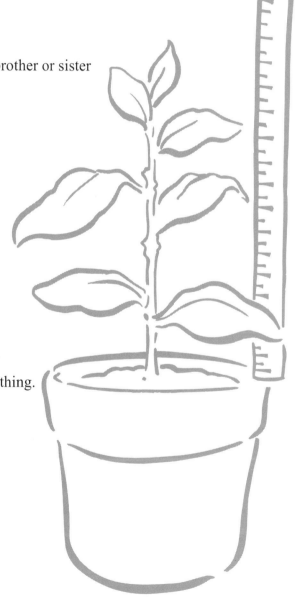

Macaroni Necklace Fun

Dye macaroni and string it to make a lovely addition to your jewelry collection.

What You Need

- package of salad macaroni
- food coloring
- rubbing alcohol
- paper towels
- long shoestring (You can to use a piece of yarn or heavy thread with a large plastic needle.)

What You Do

1. Put two tablespoons (30 ml) of rubbing alcohol in a bowl. Stir in the food coloring. (Start with six drops and vary the amount to create different colors.)

2. Add 2–4 scoops of dry macaroni. Stir until macaroni is uniformly colored.

3. Pour the macaroni onto a paper towel. Spread into a single layer. Dry for 10 minutes.

4. Make several different colors of macaroni. Store in lidded plastic containers.

5. Tie one piece of macaroni on one end of the shoestring. This will keep the macaroni from slipping off the shoestring.

6. String the macaroni. You may want to repeat a pattern or create a special colored necklace to match an outfit.

7. Wear your necklace with pride.

Outdoor Playtime

The world outside my door
Is ready to explore.
There are amazing places,
Ballgames, and fast races;
Discoveries to make,
And new pathways to take.
The world outside my door
Is ready to explore.

Play and Learn to

- learn about reflections
- invent new bubblemakers
- see how changing the shape of an object changes its performance
- create a pattern
- enlarge a design
- dig a hole
- read and follow directions
- plant and tend a minigarden
- visit new places
- sail a boat

Activities

Sun Mural

Learn about the way that light moves as you use reflections to "paint" a picture.

What You Need

- pieces of aluminum foil
- mirrors
- shiny pan lids
- scissors
- string

What You Do

1. Practice using shiny surfaces to reflect light. This will work particularly well if you find a wall in the shade with the sun directly behind it. Then you can reflect the sunlight back onto the wall.

2. Try making different-shaped reflections and moving the reflections.

3. Arrange reflective surfaces so that you create a light collage on the wall. Hang some mirrors or pieces of foil so that they move in the breeze.

4. Walk in front of a light source to create new shadows.

Parachute Party

Handkerchief parachute toys are fun and inexpensive.

What You Need

For each parachute toy:

- handkerchief (A square piece of cotton or plastic garbage bag will also work.)
- four 12" (30 cm) pieces of string
- wooden spool
- felt-tip markers

What You Do

1. Decorate the spool with markers.

2. Make the parachute from the handkerchief.
   - Pinch the corners of the handkerchief.
   - Tie a string to each corner.
   - Thread all four strings through the hole of the spool.
   - Knot the string so that the spool does not slip off.

3. Roll the parachute around the spool.

4. Toss the parachute into the air.

5. Watch the parachute float to the ground.

6. Designate a spot as the landing area and see if your parachute toys can land on the area.

Bubble Station

Invent new ways to make bubbles using things you find in your kitchen.

What You Need

- shallow pans or baking sheets
- liquid dishwashing soap
- plastic drinking straws
- electrical tape
- plastic container with a top
- glycerine (Buy it at a drugstore.)
- clean, empty cans with both ends removed

Bubble Solution

1. Fill a container with a quart (950 ml) of warm water.
2. Mix in 8 tablespoons (120 ml) of liquid soap.
3. Add 8 tablespoons (120 ml) of glycerine.
4. Stir or shake well.

What You Do

1. Assemble materials in a place where a mess won't matter. Make the bubble solution and pour it into the pans.

2. Begin by simply blowing bubbles in the pans using a drinking straw.
   - Make a giant mound of bubbles.
   - Make one big bubble dome.
   - Make a small bubble dome inside the big bubble dome.

3. Then use cups, cans, straws, and tape to create more bubbles.
   - Dip one end of a can in the bubble solution. Blow through the other end.
   - Tape several cans together and create a giant bubble.
   - Tape a handful of straws together in a bundle, dip them in the solution, and blow for an explosion of tiny bubbles.

4. Combine the cups and straws creatively to invent new ways to make bubbles.

Paper Plate Flyers

These homemade flyers help six-year-olds learn how changing the shape of something affects its performance.

What You Need

For each flyer:

• 2 paper plates the same size

• stapler

• colored markers

What You Do

1. Decorate the plates with the markers.

2. Staple the two plates together.
   - If you staple the plates back-to-back, you will create a flyer that dips and curves.
   - If you staple the plates front-to-front, you will create a flyer that flies faster and straighter.

3. Try out the flyers!

4. Think about how to change the flyers.
   What would happen if you made holes in the center or added another smaller plate on top?
   Try out your ideas.

Play and Learn with Your Six-Year-Old • EMC 4505

Fancy Fences

Decorate a fence with thin strips of plastic. It's great practice in tying!

What You Need

- a disposable plastic tablecloth or trash bag cut into thin strips (6" x 2" [15 x 5 cm])
- a fence—(A chain link fence or the side of a dog run work particularly well.)

What You Do

1. Tie strips of plastic to the fence to form shapes and designs.

2. Add details with longer strips or different colors.

3. Create a message by tying more strips in order.

Slatted fences are great for weaving. You can create a decorative weaving as a colorful backdrop for play.

Balloon Rackets

Use old nylon stockings and coat hangers to make rackets for this balloon game.

What You Need

- 2 wire coat hangers
- 2 old knee-high stockings or the leg sections cut off an old pair of pantyhose
- masking tape
- ballons

What You Do

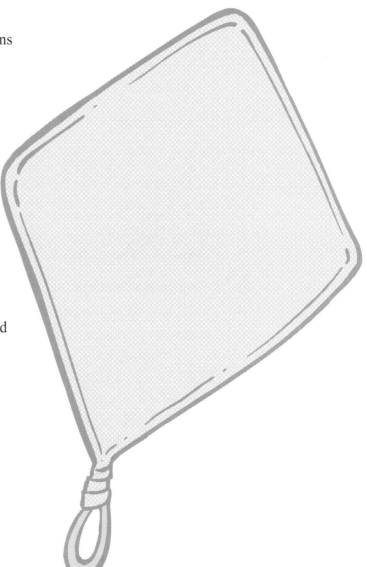

1. Pull the hangers into a diamond shape and straighten the hooks.

2. Push each hanger into a nylon stocking. Push all the way to the toe.

3. Gather the loose end by twisting it around the handle and wrapping it with tape.

4. Double the handle by bending it in half and wrapping with more tape.

5. Try balancing a balloon on the racket.

6. Use the rackets to hit a balloon back and forth.

Dig a Hole

The "whole" hole project can last for an entire summer as young excavators enjoy the challenge of digging and designing.

What You Need

- several shovels—large, small, and hand-held
- bucket
- wheelbarrow (optional)

What You Do

1. Designate a place where the hole can be dug. If you have a sandbox without a base, start there. If the area where you will dig is dry, packed soil, water thoroughly several days before the digging begins.

2. Dig! This is a good time to learn how to use a shovel.

3. Examine the differences in the soil layers as you dig. You may find what my children called "Indian clay" beneath the sandy surface. Finding a worm is an added bonus to any digging experience.

4. Young excavators may enjoy planning and designing tunnels, roads, riverways, and mountains as they dig. Encourage this creative expression. How to dispose of extra dirt is a chance for real problem solving.

Planting a Garden

Planting and tending seeds in a minigarden teaches responsibility as well as providing important experiences in science.

What You Need

- a planter box or a small garden plot
- good soil
- rocks or pieces of broken pot
- seeds
- water
- patience

What You Do

1. Prepare the soil for planting:
   - If you are using a planter, cover the bottom with rocks to ensure proper drainage and then fill the pot with soil.
   - If you are planting in a garden plot, begin by spading the soil, adding fertilizer if needed, and then raking the area to be planted.

2. Plant the seeds according to the instructions on the seed package.

3. Tend the seeds. Note the changes. Enjoy the harvest.

Choosing the seeds to plant is a big decision. Do you want flowers or vegetables? Will the garden be in the sun or the shade? Finding the answers to these real questions is a great way to encourage your six-year-old's research skills. Read seed packages together. Ask questions at the nursery. Check out a book from your library.

Outstanding Outings

Choose a place to visit with your child.

What You Need

- a destination
  (This doesn't have to be fancy. I've taken outstanding outings to the lumberyard and the neighborhood ice-cream store. The destination becomes outstanding when your focus changes. Instead of just going to the lumberyard to buy something for your home maintenance, you can plan an outing to look at different kinds of nails and discover why there are so many different kinds.)

- a time

What You Do

1. Schedule a time for your outing. Discuss a place that the two of you would like to visit.

2. Post the time and destination on your child's memoboard.

3. Go on the outing. Enjoy!

Busy lifestyles and important obligations make it hard to take outings with your six-year-old. Solve this problem by scheduling an outstanding outing once a month and then enjoy this special outdoor learning opportunity.

A Terrific Tire

An old tire ready for recycling can provide an unusual easel and then become an addition to your outdoor play equipment.

What You Need

- a tire
- several colors of water-based outdoor trim paint
- a paintbrush for each color
- a bucket of water for cleanup
- (optional) drop cloth

What You Do

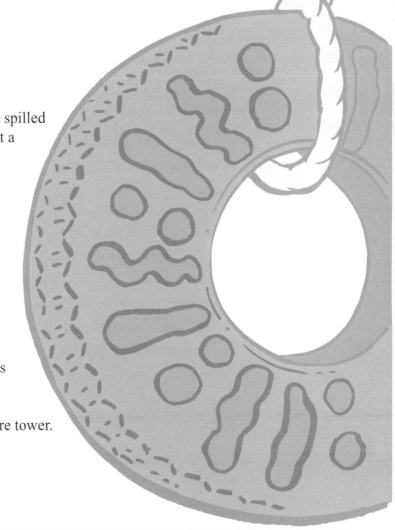

1. Set up a painting area in a place where spilled paint won't be a problem or spread out a drop cloth to catch spills.

2. Paint the tire. Be creative. Use spirals, stripes, and flowers. Paint as much of the tire as you can.

3. Let the tire dry overnight.

4. Turn the tire and paint the other side.

5. Use your new colorful tire:
   - Hang the tire to use as a throwing target.
   - Fill the tire with soil and use it as a planter box.
   - Make a tire swing.
   - Paint several tires and make a tire tower.

Silly Sailboats

Make a basic sailboat and float it in a tub of water or in the gutter on a rainy day. Then make changes to the design of the boat to improve its performance.

What You Need

- foam tray (recycled from the ones that have held food)
- sheet of paper
- scissors
- screw or nail
- straw
- tape

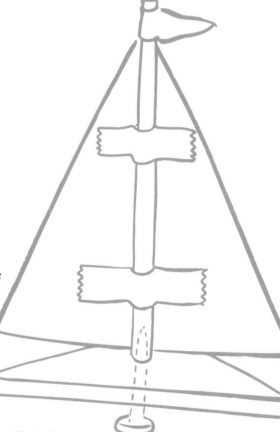

What You Do

1. Cut a small triangle from the foam tray. (This will be the boat.)

2. Cut the straw in half. Cut a triangle of paper the same height as the straw half. Tape the triangle to the straw. (This will be the sail.)

3. Attach the sail to the boat. Stick the screw or nail through the center of the triangle. Slip the straw onto the screw or nail.

4. Sail the boat in a tub of water. Blow on the sail to make the boat move faster.

5. Make changes to the design of the boat and/or the sail. Ask,
   Do the changes make the boat go faster?
   Do the changes make the boat look fancier?

Bedtime

Sing me a song.
Read and recite.
Talk and listen.
Then say, "Good night."

Bedtime Rhymes

Memorize verses and poems with your child. Recite them at bedtime and enjoy.

What You Need

• a poem, verse, or chant "in your head"

What You Do

1. When you first introduce a poem, read or recite it for your child several times. Talk about your favorite part, the rhyming words, or what it means. Invite your child to join in.

2. Say a line, then have your child repeat the line, or recite the verses and have your child recite the refrain. Learn alternating lines.

3. Enjoy the verse and then make up your own. Add finger motions. Make up a new refrain. Chant or sing the lines.

> My daughter and her friend memorized the alternate lines of *Jabberwocky* by Lewis Carroll and amazed their friends as they recited it at top speed.

Some chants and songs
to learn and enjoy.

Peanut Butter Chant

Peanut, peanut butter–jelly.
Peanut, peanut butter–jelly.

First you take the peanuts and you crush 'em, crush 'em.
First you take the peanuts and you crush 'em, crush 'em.

Peanut, peanut butter–jelly.
Peanut, peanut butter–jelly.

Next you take the grapes and you squish 'em, squish 'em.
Next you take the grapes and you squish 'em, squish 'em.

Peanut, peanut butter–jelly.
Peanut, peanut butter–jelly.

Then you take the bread and you slice it, slice it.
Then you take the bread and you slice it, slice it.

Peanut, peanut butter–jelly.
Peanut, peanut butter–jelly.

Next you take the knife and you spread it, spread it.
Next you take the knife and you spread it, spread it.

Peanut, peanut butter–jelly.
Peanut, peanut butter–jelly.

Now you take the slices and you slap 'em, slap 'em.
Now you take the slices and you slap 'em, slap 'em.

Peanut, peanut butter–jelly.
Peanut, peanut butter–jelly.

Take that special sandwich and bite it, bite it.
Take that special sandwich and bite it, bite it.

(As if your mouth is full of sticky peanut butter)
Peanut, peanut butter–jelly.
Peanut, peanut butter–jelly.

Up to the Ceiling Handshake

Up to the ceiling,
Down to the floor.

Left to the window,
Right to the door.

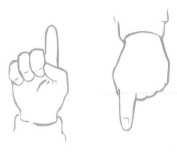

This is *my* right hand—
Raise it up high.

This is *my* left hand—
Reach for the sky.

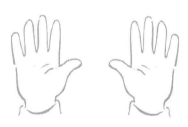

Right hand, left hand,
Twirl them 'round.

Left hand, right hand,
Shake up an' down.

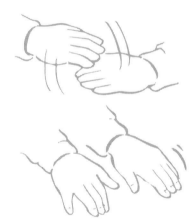

This Old Man

This old man, he played one.
He played knick-knack on his thumb.

Refrain:
With a knick-knack, paddy whack,
Give your dog a bone.
This old man came rolling home.

This old man, he played two.
He played knick-knack on his shoe.

This old man, he played six.
He played knick-knack on two sticks.

This old man, he played three.
He played knick-knack on his knee.

This old man, he played seven.
He played knick-knack up to heaven.

This old man, he played four.
He played knick-knack on my door.

This old man, he played eight.
He played knick-knack on the gate.

This old man, he played five.
He played knick-knack on the hive.

This old man, he played nine.
He played knick-knack on my spine.

This old man, he played ten.
He played knick-knack once again.

Six Little Ducks Song

Six little ducks

That I once knew.

Fat ducks, skinny ducks,

Fair ducks, too.

But the one little duck

With a feather on its back,

It led the others with

A quack, quack, quack.

Down to the river

They would go,

Wibble-wobble, wibble-wobble,

To and fro.

But the one little duck

With a feather on its back,

It led the others with

A quack, quack, quack!

Quack, quack, quack.

Quack, quack, quack.

It led the others with a quack,
quack, quack!

Play and Learn with Your Six-Year-Old • EMC 4505

Something Happened

Use quiet moments as you tuck your child into bed to think of the important things that have happened during the day.

What You Need

- a quiet time
- a notebook

What You Do

1. Ask your child to tell about something important that happened during the day.

2. Listen as your child responds. Be sure to find out why an event is considered important. The explanation often is the most important part of the conversation.

3. Using your child's words, record and date the event. This book may help you to identify your child's special interests, understand your child's relationships with friends, and discover your child's learning style.

> When you ask your child to tell about important things and to explain why those things are important, you engage your child in critical thinking and evaluation.

October

Today we went to the pumpkin farm. We brought home one big pumpkin and two

A Penny a Day

This simple activity will help your child learn that different coins have equivalent values.

What You Need

- 10 pennies
- 2 dimes
- 2 fifty-cent pieces
- dollar bills
- coin purse
- 2 nickels
- 2 quarters
- silver dollar
- see-through container

What You Do

1. Put the money in the coin purse and designate it as the "bank."

2. Each night put one penny in the see-through container.

3. Then dump the container out and count to determine the value of the coins.

4. Each time several coins can be replaced with a single coin, make the trade.
   - 5 pennies should be traded for 1 nickel
   - 2 nickels should be traded for 1 dime

5. When you "save" $1, decide together on a special way to spend that dollar.

Shadow Fun

Make shadows on the wall of the bedroom and you can learn about several important properties of light.

What You Need

- flashlight
- small objects

What You Do

1. Use the flashlight and an object to make a shadow on the wall.

2. Change the shadow by moving the object or the light. Your child will soon recognize that a shadow is made when an object blocks a light source and that shadows change size when the distance between the object and the light source changes.

3. Enjoy more shadow play.
    - Use your hand to create animal-shaped shadows. Make the animals carry on a conversation.
    - Make simple shadow puppets (figures attached to a straw) and use them to present a play. Have your child tell the story and use the puppets to act it out.

Read Frank Asch's *Bear Shadow* (Prentice Hall, 1985) some night after your shadow fun and laugh with your child about Bear's shadow problems.

While-You-Wait Time

I practice my adding,
Measure, and estimate,
And then I just imagine.
Now isn't that great.
Don't worry. It's o.k.
If you have to be late.
I won't waste a minute.
I can learn while I wait.

Play and Learn to

- identify attributes of objects
- practice adding and subtracting
- learn about measuring
- practice problem-solving strategies
- locate words in text
- expand vocabulary

Activities

Fortunately, Unfortunately

Enjoy this story-creating experience together as you play this no-equipment-needed game.

What You Need

• time to think

What You Do

1. Take turns creating a story that begins with a fortunate event.

   Fortunately the sun was shining.

2. Continue with an unfortunate event in the story.

   Unfortunately the flowers were thirsty.

3. Alternate fortunate and unfortunate events until the story ends.

   Fortunately Chelsea had a watering can full of water.

   Unfortunately she tripped and spilled the water on the driveway.

   Fortunately the water ran down the driveway to the flowers.

   Unfortunately Chelsea skinned her knee when she fell.

   Fortunately Daddy was home to kiss it better.

   The End

How Many?

This simple game of hide-and-seek with pennies helps six-year-olds add and subtract.

What You Need

- some pennies
- a hand

What You Do

1. Show four pennies in your hand. Identify the number.

2. Take three pennies out of your hand and put them in your child's hand. Close your hand to "hide" the remaining penny.

3. Have your child tell how many pennies he or she has.

4. Keeping your hand closed, ask,
   How many pennies do I have?

5. If your child doesn't know, open your hand and show.

6. Repeat using different numbers of pennies.

7. Have your child hold the pennies originally and transfer some to your hand, asking you to identify how many are left.

Inchworm Measuring

Use a piece of paper to make an inchworm. Then measure the things around you using the inchworm.

What You Need

- a piece of paper
- an object to measure

What You Do

1. Crush the paper into a wad. Flatten the wad into a cylindrical shape to make the inchworm.

2. Measure something around you using the inchworm as the unit of measure. Start at one end of the object. Show your child how to use a finger to mark the spot and move the worm forward.

3. After you have measured several objects, try estimating the size of an object before you measure it.
Then measure to see if you were close.

4. Encourage your child to compare objects measured. Ask,

   What was longer, the magazine or my purse?
   Is the table wider than the chair?

Build a Bridge

Discover that some shapes are stronger than other shapes as you practice problem solving.

What You Need

• an index card (A reply card from a magazine will work.)

What You Do

1. Lay the card between two objects to make a bridge.

2. Test the strength of the bridge by placing one penny on it. Ask,
   Can the bridge hold more than one penny?
   How many pennies can it hold before it collapses?

3. Challenge your child to change the bridge so that it will be stronger. Try for multiple solutions.

4. Let your child test to see if the bridge is stronger.

5. When you see real bridges, check for any similarities between them and your card bridge.
   Are there differences?

   Does looking at real bridges give you any ideas for changes that might make your bridge stronger?

I Collect Words

For creating while waiting, carry a small notebook with a pencil.

What You Need

- a small notebook—a memo-sized spiral one is great
- a pencil
- a string

What You Do

1. Attach the pencil to the notebook.

2. Carry the notebook in your purse or pocket so that it is always handy.

3. Have your child copy words from the print around you.

4. Your child may choose to draw pictures to show what the word is. The notebook then becomes a minipicture dictionary.

5. Date the pages and you'll be able to remember where you were waiting on a certain day.

Later, the notebook of words can be used as a reference for writing.

Cross It Out!

Use any print source handy as a game board.

What You Need

- a church bulletin, an advertising flyer, or a newspaper
- pencil or highlighter

What You Do

1. Pick a simple word or letter.

2. Take turns with your child:
   - locate the word or letter in the print
   - highlight or cross out the word

3. Count the number of times you located the word or letter.

Travel Time

Going to the store,
Biking down the street,
Going to Grandma's in Mom's
backseat,
Riding on a bus,
Sleeping on a train,
Flying through the clouds on a
big jet plane—
I'm traveling!

Play and Learn to

- identify letters
- group things in categories
- sing songs
- read familiar words
- think creatively
- compare objects
- read a map
- use letter clues to read words

Activities

Alphabet Billboards

As you travel in a car watch the signs going by to find all the letters of the alphabet.

What You Need

• a variety of billboards or direction signs

What You Do

1. Start with **A.**

2. Find the letter on a sign outside the window of your vehicle.

3. Look for a **B.**

4. Work your way through the whole alphabet. Often a sign will have more than one letter on it.

Read-my-World Bingo

Make a bingo card using travel brochures and ticket folders. As you move through an airline terminal or national park, your child can "collect" the print to score a bingo.

What You Need

- a lightweight piece of cardboard
- advertisements, brochures, and pamphlets
- scissors
- glue
- clear contact paper

What You Do

1. Before you go on the trip, work with your child to make a bingo card using the print that you might see as you travel.
   - Draw a grid on a lightweight piece of cardboard. Mark the middle space FREE.
   - Cut words and pictures from advertisements, brochures, and pamphlets.
   - Paste the cutouts on the grid to make the bingo card.
   - Cover the card with clear contact paper.

2. As you travel, look for the print. Use an erasable pen to circle the words that you find.

3. Yell "Bingo" when you find 5 in a row.

All Fish Swim

This is a beginning category game that may cause giggles.

What You Need

• several general categories—animals that swim, flying animals, things with wheels

What You Do

1. Choose a category.
   animals that swim

2. Take turns naming things that fit in that category.
   Goldfish swim.
   Whales swim.
   Ducks swim.

3. When you or your child can't think of a thing that fits in the category, try a silly response.
   Refrigerators swim.

4. Start a new category with the next response.

Dot-to-Dot Doodling

Create your own creative dot-to-dot pictures. See how creative you can be.

What You Need

- paper
- pencil

What You Need

1. Give your child a piece of paper and keep one for yourself. Make 25 dots on the paper. Put the dots anywhere on the page.

2. Exchange pages.

3. Look at all the dots. Try to imagine a way to connect them to make a picture. Turn the paper around to see the dots in different ways.

4. Connect the dots so that a picture emerges. There is no right answer to this activity. Celebrate unusual solutions.

5. Try more dots. Try fewer dots.

I Wonder... Journal

Record questions in a journal anytime you or your child wonder something. Use travel time to discuss possible answers to the questions posed.

What You Need

• a small notebook

• a pencil

What You Do

1. Get a notebook and keep it handy.

2. When your child asks a "Why?" question or wonders about something, record it in the notebook.

3. Add some musings of your own:
   I wonder what would happen if horses could talk.
   I wonder what would happen if it didn't rain for a whole year.

I wonder why birds don't fall out of trees when they sleep

Ten Guesses

Try this variation of the traditional game of Hangman. Six-year-olds love to use what they know about letters and words to solve a puzzle.

What You Need

- paper
- pencil

What You Do

1. Think of a simple sentence. It's better if the sentence is true and relevant to your child.
   Today is Grammy's birthday.

2. Draw a short line for each letter in the sentence. Leave spaces between the words.

   _ _ _ _ _ _ _ _ _ _ _ _ _ ' _ _ _ _ _ _ _ _ _ .

3. Your child guesses letters, one at a time, that might be in the sentence.

4. Write in letters that are correct. Write the letters that are incorrect on the side of the paper.

5. See how quickly your child can read the sentence.

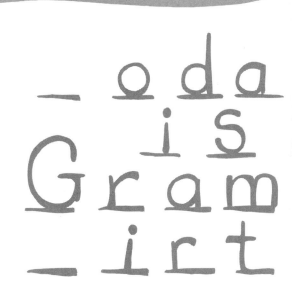

Reading a Map

Your child's questions *"Are we there yet?"* and *"How much farther?"* become learning experiences when you have taken the time to develop these basic map skills.

What You Need

several maps:

• a map of your neighborhood
(Your phone book may include this map.
Look to see.)

• a map of the area where you are traveling

• a map of the world

What You Do

1. Begin by helping your child identify the location of your street on the neighborhood map. Look for the locations of other familiar places—the grocery store, the school, your church, the neighborhood park, the library. Trace the route you would take to travel to one of these places. Then actually travel the route, consulting the map often.

2. Look at the map of the area where you are traveling. Locate your home and your destination. Identify landmarks in between. As you travel note your progress on the map.

3. Finally, look at the map of the world. Locate your home. Discuss the locations of places that are in the news. Pin the map to a bulletin board or wall and mark locations.

Story Time

Once upon a time
In a kingdom far away,
I spent a million hours
Telling stories all the day.
There were princes, brave kings,
And a great hall with a fire,
Talking frogs, and a princess
Everyone could admire.

Play and Learn to

- tell and retell stories
- predict what will happen next
- sequence story events
- make and use puppets
- write words, sentences, and stories
- make a book
- produce a play

Activities

Shared Reading

Sit with your child on your lap or snuggle together on the sofa and share a favorite book.

What You Need

• a good book

What You Do

1. Read with feeling.

2. Let your child participate by:
   filling in words
   turning pages
   pointing out pictures
   talking about the story

A Few Suggestions:

Bookstores and libraries are filled with wonderful books for you and your child to share. There are a number of excellent read-aloud guides that will help you choose good literature appropriate to the age of your child. Buy a few special books to enjoy over and over again at bedtime. Visit your library often to choose new books to read.

This is my teddy
He has a crown
and I love him.

A Note about Reading

The most important thing you can do for your child is **read**.

Read to your child. Read yourself so that your child sees you reading.

Read books, signs, labels, letters, directions, and displays.

Visit libraries and bookstores. Read your way through museums, parks, stores, and playgrounds. Remember that any time of day is a good time to read.

Reading Stories

Practice important prereading skills as you read.

What You Need

• a story book

What You Do

1. Retell the story.

   Your child's ability to retell, to summarize, and to order the events in a story are indicators of reading readiness. When you have finished reading a story, ask your child to tell what the story was about.

2. Predict what will happen next.

   Stop reading and ask your child to predict what will happen next. Listen carefully and then read on to see if the prediction was correct.

3. Sequence events in a story.

   Read the story. Identify with your child the important things that happened in the story. Have your child draw a picture or write a word on an index card to represent each thing. Put the cards in order to show the sequence of events.

4. Extend the story.

   After you have finished reading, ask your child to make up a new adventure for the characters in the story or think of a different ending. Write the adventure or keyboard it as your child tells it. Add pictures and a cover. You can start your own set of stories.

Flip Books

Make a flip book and create new characters. Then tell or write stories about them.

What You Need

- 3 sheets of 8½" x 11" (21 x 28 cm) paper
- crayons or marking pens
- stapler

What You Do

1. Fold the sheets of paper in half to make long, thin rectangles.

2. Cut the papers along the fold line to make six long, narrow pages.

3. Fold each narrow page into thirds. Unfold.

4. Draw a character on each page following these directions:
   - On the top third, draw a hat.
   - On the middle third, draw a face.
   - On the bottom third, draw a collar or neck.

5. Stack the six pages together. Staple them on the left side.

6. Carefully cut along the fold lines almost to the stapled edge so that you can flip one portion of the page without turning the rest of the page.

7. Flip the different parts of the pages to make new characters.

8. Tell or write a story about the characters you create.

Play and Learn with Your Six-Year-Old • EMC 4505

A Writing Box

Keep a writing supply box ready so that you can make writing a part of your everyday routine.

What You Need

- a box
- paper (several different kinds)
- pens, pencils, markers, crayons
- small notebook
- envelopes

What You Do

1. Have your child help put the materials for the writing box together.

2. Encourage your child to write often. The best encouragement may be a shared writing time with both of you sitting and writing. Say,
   Let's write a letter to Grandma.

3. Offer to write captions on pictures that your child has drawn. Include his or her signature on letters that you are sending. Write down stories as they are told and have your child draw illustrations.

Rebus Stories

Combine pictures and words to write a rebus story. Then collect the stories to make a book.

What You Need

- paper
- pencil, crayons, marking pens
- a source of pictures—magazines, comic strips, advertisements
- scissors

What You Do

1. With your child, cut ten pictures from the picture sources.

2. Begin writing a story, "Once there was a…" (paste the picture in place of the word).

3. Continue writing and pasting until the story is complete and all ten pictures have been used. Some of your characters may have to "do" some unusual things so that you can use each of the pictures, but that's part of the fun!

Producing a Play

Whether your production includes costumes and programs or simply applause, a play is a wonderful creative outlet for six-year-olds.

What You Need

- imagination

The following items are optional:

- costumes
- props
- a script
- a curtain

What You Do

1. Talk with your child about what a play is.
   Explain that actors pretend to be the characters in a story.
   Take your child to see a real play if possible.

2. Put on your own production.
   - Choose a familiar story with repeating actions such as *Caps for Sale* by Espher Slobodkina.
   - Select roles. Prepare costumes. (This is optional. The costumes can be imaginary.)
   - Retell the story and act it out. Practice several times and then do your play for an audience.

3. Gradually choose more complicated stories and make your productions more involved.

Happy Hopper

**Make this stick puppet to use in your next puppet production.
You may want to create a whole family.**

What You Need

- toilet paper roll
- paper towel, crumpled into a ball
- plastic wiggle eyes
- broomstraw
- pipe cleaners
- glue
- pencil or thin dowel

What You Do

1. Stick the crumpled paper towel into the end of the toilet paper roll to make the head.

2. Glue short pieces of broomstraw to the head for antennae.

3. Glue the wiggle eyes to the head.

4. Bend pipe cleaners into grasshopper leg shapes. Glue to the body.

5. Stick the pencil or thin dowel through the bottom of the grasshopper's body.

6. Make the grasshopper hop and leap.

Flyswatter Puppet

A simple flyswatter becomes a friendly character.

What You Need

- flyswatter
- felt or paper scraps
- 12" (30 cm) length of fat yarn or thin rope
- glue

What You Do

1. Glue felt or paper eyes, nose, mouth, and other features to the flyswatter.

2. Tie yarn around the handle for arms.

3. Use your puppet to give directions on how to do something.

All about Me

**Record your child's thoughts and stories. Add pictures
to create a special book of remembrances.**

What You Need

- a computer or traditional writing tools
- paper
- photos or child-drawn illustrations
- a scrapbook

What You Do

1. Copy a thought or a story down as your child
   tells it.

2. Take photos or draw pictures to illustrate the text.

3. Mount the text and illustrations on scrapbook pages.
   Note the date the page was created and any other
   interesting circumstances. Your scrapbook will become
   an important keepsake.

4. Read and enjoy.

We went t[o]
Pool and
to Swim

June

     Play and Learn with Your Six-Year-Old • EMC 4505